ON B

A QUAKER

MEMBERSHIP:

past – present – future

ALASTAIR HERON

Curlew Productions
Kelso • Scotland
2000

ACKNOWLEDGMENTS

First, to Elsa Dicks and Beth Allen, who back in September 1998 aroused my interest in having a fresh look at membership, its meaning and the way that we deal with it. None of us could foresee that the subject would be addressed at Yearly Meeting 2000, and work on this book was well advanced before that was decided.

Then to Josef Keith at Friends House Library, and Mary Jo Clegg at Woodbrooke Library, for their essential help as I sought to trace the evolution of membership through 350 years. My thanks also to Peggy Morscheck, Director of the Quaker Information Center, Philadelphia for her valuable assistance, especially regarding Philadelphia Yearly Meeting.

Next to the three readers of my first draft: David Barkla, Barbara Bowman and Jane Muers. They all effected improvements, but cannot be held responsible for the defects of the published version.

And finally, a long overdue expression of gratitude to David and Fran Woolgrove, publishers and supportive friends through the years. They have made my literary endeavours an adventure instead of a burden.

Contents

The Quaker objection to credal statements is not to beliefs as such, but to the use of an officially-sanctioned selection of them to improve a uniformity in things where the gospel proclaims freedom. 'Credo' is the Latin for 'I believe'. The meaning of the word is debased if you confine it to an act of the will giving intellectual assent to articles of faith. It is much better translated as 'I commit myself to...' in the sense that one is prepared to take the full consequences of the beliefs one has adopted.[1]

This short book on Quaker membership in Britain is intended to fill a gap. Most Friends today are unaware of the evolution of Quaker membership, from the time of George Fox until the present day. So some blithely ask why we need membership at all, when it was not formally established until the early seventeen-hundreds; and an unknown proportion might have to plead ignorance of the precise conditions under which it is now acquired.

There is obviously a close connection between the concept of 'identity' and that of 'membership'. The latter is about 'being part of, committed to', while the former answers the questions 'of what?' and 'to what?' Any substantial uncertainty about identity creates difficulties about membership. Here in Britain our Quaker identity is now hard to define, as diversity of personal belief has tended to become a corporate virtue. Those in membership struggle to say what it means in terms of their own faith position, while those contemplating the possibility of becoming members may wonder what they would be joining.

This book has been written against that background. The evolution of Quaker membership is traced from the time of Fox to 1993. Then our 'present' is reviewed, first as defined by our 'Book of Christian discipline', and then in terms of our continuing inability to replace ourselves. A personal approach to future action on both these fronts constitutes the second half of the book.

The historical chapter is essentially factual, with a minimum of selection. The review of the present situation, while wholly factual about recruitment to membership, is selective in the approach to its meaning as set out in " Quaker faith and practice", and not all topics are addressed. In 'The future', the author feels free to write in the first person singular – to say what he feels and thinks about our situation, and how to tackle it. The meaning of membership among British Quakers was considered carefully by two end-on review committees over a thirteen-year period in the 1970s and 1980s to almost no effect. But the topic will not go away, is in fact becoming pressing: so the more individual Friends and their meetings can be persuaded to wrestle with it, the better for the future of Quakers in Britain. If this study proves useful in that process, one 'ancient Quaker' will be glad.

The Past
1647 to 1993

Before formal membership

For ninety years from 1647 to 1737 there was no formal membership, or procedure for acquiring it. But probably sixty thousand adults in England 'became Quakers' before 1700. How did they do it? The answer is not to be found in the minutes of London Yearly Meeting from its establishment in 1678, or even in the 1782 "Book of extracts[2]" (retrospective to the same date) which laid the foundation for what we now know as the 'Book of discipline'. But answer there is, more than enough to deal with such questions as 'There was no membership among early Friends, so why do we have to have it now?'

Right from the beginning, most local groups of active Quakers attracted those whom we would today describe as 'Attenders'. Although left free to describe themselves publicly as 'Quakers' if they wished, they were not recognised as such by the meeting until it became clear that they had experienced 'convincement', and were also engaged upon 'the necessary work of conversion'. During at least the first fifty years, the term 'convincement' was not used in its intellectual sense, but to mean 'conviction' of sin – of having 'missed the mark' – and a turning to the Light of Christ within. It was seen as the first step on the road to 'conversion', the experience of being changed, of progress, often slow and painful, to full acceptance of God's dominion in one's life.

Francis Howgill wrote in 1658 'A man unconverted yet convinced is still in darkness', and in 1692 John Banks spelled it out in detail thus: 'Because you are "convinced" of the "Truth," and because you know the "Truth" and "Way" of "God", what it is and so make a "Profession" thereof; think not that this "knowledge" will serve your turn to justify you in the sight of God, short of "Obedience".' And 'Those who are obedient come to know not only a "convinced estate", but a "conversion" in their hearts and souls.' In his "Apology"[3] Robert Barclay wrote the words made familiar by their inclusion in *Quaker faith and practice*, the current book of discipline of what is now Britain Yearly Meeting :

> *Not by strength of arguments or by a particular disquisition of each doctrine, and convincement of my understanding thereby, came I to receive and bear witness of the Truth, but by being secretly reached by the Life. For when I came into the silent assemblies of God's people, I felt a secret power among them, which touched my heart, and as I gave way unto it I found the evil weakening in me and the good raised up; and so I became thus knit and united unto them, hungering more and more after the increase of this power and life whereby I might feel myself perfectly redeemed; and indeed this is the surest way to become a Christian... (19.21)*

(When British Quakers today have occasion to refer to this extract, they usually omit the first sentence, and stop with the words 'the good raised up').

In the 1803 revision of the "Book of extracts" there is a 1710 reference which makes clear how the distinction was to be used in pastoral practice: 'We esteem it very necessary that young, convinced and well-inclined persons and friends (*sic*) be early visited in the love of God, by faithful Friends, for their encouragement, help and furtherance in the Truth'. When newcomers reached the point where they not only came regularly to the meetings for worship, but also made it clear in their speech and behaviour that they were in unity with Quaker profession and practice, they began to be recognised as 'convinced persons'. Following the establishment by George Fox in 1667 of a hierarchy of business meetings, anchored in the Monthly Meetings, the need arose to decide who was eligible to take part in their work. Such eligibility did not automatically include those perceived as 'convinced persons'.

At first, there was usually no difficulty, since seasoned well-established Friends were available for service. In due course, it became necessary to identify other possibly suitable participants. Vann[4] cites Robert Barclay (of Reigate, not the Apologist) as holding that 'the "convinced" were always and only those who formed a kind of "outside membership" in early Quakerism, enjoying the right to be relieved in necessity, *while the "converted" had… the right of sitting in the business meetings'* [present emphasis]. Evidence for this is to be found, not always consistently, in Monthly Meeting minutes of the period. But it certainly raises the question 'How did a "convinced person" become recognised as being "converted" ?', to which the answer is 'Sometimes by public profession, and subsequent acceptance, within the Meeting, more often by tacit recognition, accompanied by an invitation to sit in the business meetings'. An application to be married according to Quaker usage frequently gave rise to a careful enquiry into the progress along the road to conversion of the two parties involved.

But given the difficulty a meeting might face in deciding upon the reality of a person's conversion, it is unsurprising that emphasis was placed upon what were known as the 'testimonies' – in other words, on the person's public behaviour. The principal requirements were plain dress; refusal to accord 'hat honour', or to swear an oath; the use of 'thou' instead of the customary 'you'; and a steadfast refusal to pay tithes to the Established Church. To these 'testimonies' must be added avoidance of drunkenness (not requiring total abstinence); honesty both in personal relations and in trade or business; no running into debt; not getting married 'before a priest'; nor living as if married with a person not their wife or husband.

As early as 1666 the term 'member' was used, as for example in the epistle from the Yearly Meeting of Ministers in that year, which referred to 'members of the church'. Even in that early period, the term 'disownment' was occasionally used of someone who had been accepted by the meeting as a Quaker, but had then 'run out' in his or her behaviour and was unrepentant about it. Repentance was usually evidenced by the writing of a statement by the offender, condemning the behaviour, and making it available not only to the meeting, but to all parties involved or whom the behaviour affected. As noted by Punshon[5], 'this procedure was designed to "clear Truth", not to humiliate the offender. It provided the Society with an opportunity to "disown" disorderly conduct. It is extremely rare for the record books to reveal any disciplinary proceeding about matters of doctrine.'

Refusal to make this public statement would lead the meeting to minute the facts of the case, and to refer to the person concerned as 'one reputed to be a Quaker', but who was not perceived by them as one.

Recognising that *acceptance* as a Quaker – and *continuance* as part of the Quaker community – was no easy matter, mention also must be made of the potential cost of *identifying* oneself with them, during the periods of persecution. The first was under the Protectorate from 1653 to 1660, and then – more severely – after the Restoration of the monarchy, until relief came with the accession of James II and then more fully with the Toleration Act of 1689. Braithwaite[6] estimated that 'the total number of Quaker sufferers, by imprisonment and otherwise, in England and Wales during the Restoration period considerably exceeded 15,000 ... (of whom) at least 450 died under their sufferings.'

It seems clear that during the ninety years preceding the establishment of formal membership, a virtual form of it obtained: *local Quakers knew who was a Quaker, and who was not.* An important, but not the only visible sign was inclusion without question in the meetings for worship for business. On the pastoral side, there is evidence that active support was given to those on the road from being 'merely convinced' to 'knowing a conversion in their hearts and souls'.

The 'Rules of settlement' 1737

This decisive event has been well described by Punshon[7]

> *A number of attempts to codify Friends' practice were made before Yearly Meeting in 1737 issued nine guidelines that effectively settled matters, and inadvertently started the institution of birthright membership. It ruled that* (inter alia) *: (1) All were to be deemed members of the quarterly or two-weeks meeting within the area of which they resided on 1 June 1737; (2) monthly meetings were to be responsible for the relief of Friends in want, except those who were properly in the charge of some other meeting; (3) to minimise disagreement under the second head, Friends had to have a certificate before they moved,*

addressed to the monthly meeting of the area to which they were going; (4) if they were accepted (it seems) there had to be a three years' residence before complete responsibility passed from the old to the new meeting; (5) wives and children were deemed members of their husband's or father's meeting.

It is interesting to note that to this day the Discipline of London Yearly Meeting does not provide for "automatic transfer". It would be in perfectly right ordering for one monthly meeting to grant a certificate of removal but for another with good reason to refuse it.

The most important point to note about these rules is that they did not address themselves to the problem of "who" was a member, but to "where" membership was held.

...all sects have the problem of how to extend membership to children, who have not had the fiery convincement of the first generation. The Quakers simply sidestepped the problem by enrolling children by virtue of their birth ... That can not have been the intention in 1737, but it was certainly the effect. It shifted the whole basis of oversight and pastoral care to the family, rather than the individual, with everything that entailed. The first and most obvious effect was that ... there grew up a class of habitual birthright Quakers, distinguished by adherence rather than commitment ... by 1750 the overwhelming majority of Friends, perhaps eighty per cent, were birthright members. pp. 134/5]

If guideline (1) is considered against the background of the previous discussion on 'membership', it is at once apparent that every meeting was obliged in 1737 to decide who were to be identified as being covered by that guideline.

In the absence of evidence to the contrary, the most likely criterion was current acceptance in the business meeting.

The 'Discipline' after 1737

In the original [1782] "Book of extracts" we find this, taken from an advice from Yearly Meeting in 1753:

> *And that Friends be careful to lay hands suddenly on no man, but distinguish between a true Christian tenderness to help the weak, and an hasty unreserved reception of those under convincement into membership with us; which has often hurt the particulars, by settling them in a false rest, and been very injurious to the reputation of the Society.*

This advice was either extended or replaced by one issued in 1764, as follows:

> *Advised that monthly or two-weeks meetings lay hands on no man suddenly nor speedily admit any, who come to Friends meetings as convinced persons, into membership; especially such as discover an earnestness for a speedy admission into communion with us, without a seasonable time to consider their conduct. Let the innocency of their lives and conversation first be manifested, and let a deputation of judicious Friends be made, to enquire into the sincerity of their convincement of the truth of our religious principles, and let this appear to the satisfaction of the monthly meeting, previous to their admission.*

These advices – which appear to have been the first on this subject, including the establishment of the process of 'visitation' still operative today – provide support for the view that the 18th century found Quakers retreating behind their hedge. They serve to make it clear that they had become concerned about their corporate reputation, and that suitability for admission to membership had become as much a matter of proper Quaker behaviour, as one based mainly on evidence that the applicants 'knew a conversion in their hearts and souls'.

It was not until 1812 that the yearly meeting required monthly meetings to keep an alphabetical list of their members, although some meetings had responded to earlier calls for lists.

There is scanty evidence during the 18th century about what we would today call 'outreach', as the Society increasingly relied upon enough of its birthright members remaining within the fold to sustain its business and pastoral processes. In 1726 an explicit query about the numbers convinced [*sic*] during the course of the last year was added to the old question 'How has Truth prospered among you since the last Yearly Meeting?' Quoting from Vann[8].

> *The answers returned to this query during the first thirty years show that in only two of these thirty years did as many as half the meetings reporting say that there was some convincement during the past year; in several years three-quarters or even four-fifths of the meetings reported very little, if any, convincement. [p.167]*

There were however regional differences. Yorkshire, Lancashire, Westmorland and Cumberland made positive returns in most years. Contrasting with Norwich, Colchester, Bristol, Surrey and the Midlands, which could only report new members in less than five of the thirty years reviewed. During the next 100 years to 1856 it would appear that membership was rarely on the agenda. By then the adult membership of London Yearly Meeting was less than 14,000 - the lowest in its history. In his famous 'prize essay', John Stephenson Rowntree[9] identified as prime cause the practice of disowning members who got 'married before a priest'. But he also observed that '...Friends have greatly erred in maintaining (silent waiting on God) as the only form of worship which He accepts, and from its being adapted only to certain orders and conditions of mind, the character of public worship, as it is now ordinarily presented in the meetings of the Friends, constitutes an important cause of the fewness of their numbers.'

With what for today's Quakers may seem almost indecent haste, the yearly meeting in 1861 approved a revision of the Discipline. This abolished disownment for 'marriage before a priest', and made many other changes: but it made no mention of adult membership, or of procedures for its acquisition. Still firmly founded on birthright membership, the Revision referred to the need for encouragement to the children of members - but did add 'and of attenders'.

The first small breakthrough came in 1883, when a fresh revision produced a book of discipline in three parts – Christian doctrine; Christian practice; and Church government. The 1764 advice already quoted above was retained in the last, followed by:

> *Whilst all who are drawn to unite with us in sincerity should be welcomed in a spirit of Christian kindness and cordiality, we greatly desire that a loving care may be exercised that all such are not only satisfied of the true grounds of our distinguishing Christian principles, but are also giving evidence of conversion of heart, and of love to our Lord and Saviour.*

The last few words may well reflect the strong 'evangelical' influences in London Yearly Meeting during the 19th century, but the main thrust takes us right back to the importance of the difference between convincement and conversion. This signals a fresh start for the acquisition of adult membership.

The Friends Home Missions Committee

This committee presented a substantial report to the 1899 Yearly Meeting concerning Attenders, of which the following passage is germane to our present purpose:

> *There are still left points of vital importance about which Monthly Meeting committees should satisfy themselves. The chief of these are that the applicant has experienced a change of heart, and given evidence of it in his life; and that he appreciates our religious principles as far as understood. It may further be of great service to ascertain if the applicant has sought for and felt the guidance of the Holy Spirit in the step he has taken.*

This report was well-received by the Yearly Meeting, and in the absence of any other explicit provision, the quoted extract may have influenced visitors and monthly meetings as they considered applications for membership during the ensuing years. It came only four years after the Manchester Conference, and during the height of the activities of John Wilhelm Rowntree and others, which included the start of the Summer Schools in Yorkshire and the founding of Woodbrooke College in Selly Oak.

Surprisingly, nothing appears to have happened in relation to membership, or the way in which it was approached through the Discipline or otherwise, for more than thirty years. During and after the 1914-1918 war many were drawn to the Quaker position on peace and pacifism, some of whom came into membership of the Society. During the 1920s the subject came up on several occasions, and this contributed to the slowly growing feeling that there was further work to be done on *Church Government*, even though it had been revised in 1906 and again in 1917.

The 1931 Revision of Church Government[10]

We now break new ground, for this is the first occasion upon which the Discipline contains a full section on Membership, including 'advice to visitors'. This was recognised by the provision, not only of a Preface and an Introduction, but also of the Introduction to the 1834 edition of the Discipline, entitled 'On the origin of the Christian discipline established among Friends'. A short quotation from this will serve to underline what has already been noted about the concept of membership among the early Quakers:

> *Being thus separated from others, and many being every day added to the Church, there arose, of course, peculiar duties of the associated persons towards each other. Christianity has ever been a powerful, active, and beneficent principle. Those who truly receive it no more 'live unto themselves', and this feature and fruit of genuine Christianity was strikingly exhibited in the conduct of the early Friends. No sooner were a few persons connected together in the new bond of religious fellowship, than they were engaged to admonish, encourage, and, in spiritual as well as temporal matters, to watch over and help one another in love.*
>
> *The members who lived near to each other, and who met together for religious worship, immediately formed, from the very law of their union, a Christian family or Church. **Each member was at liberty to exercise the gift bestowed upon him, in that beautiful harmony and subjection which belong to the several parts of a living body,** from the analogy to which the apostle Paul draws so striking*

a description of the true Church: 'Ye are the body of
Christ, and members in particular.' [present emphasis]

This sense of a faith community is picked up and expressed
in different terms a century later in the 1931 Introduction:

They had an intense sense of the deep meaning of
membership one with another as fellow disciples of
Christ, and of there being a place and a function for
each one in the life of the Church. They came to see,
too, that it helps the individual disciple in his task of
following the Divine Guide to share his experience with
his fellow members and to seek their sense of guidance
to aid his own. Thus the organization of the Society of
Friends has developed to express this membership, to
give opportunities for these functions to every member,
*and **to encourage the individual, the group and***
the whole Society to seek and find the guidance
of the Spirit of Christ, as the Lord and the
leader of all His disciples.

While it is easy to detect in the 1834 quotation the current
influence of 'evangelical' Friends in London Yearly Meeting,
that cannot serve as an explanation for the uncompromising
affirmation in the 1931 Introduction. The 'Spirit' was
unequivocally that of the inward Christ, and 'every member
was at liberty to exercise the gift bestowed upon him'
through seeking and finding 'the guidance of the Spirit of
Christ, as the Lord and the leader of all His disciples'.

We now move on 36 years to see what happened on the
next occasion.

The 1967 Church Government

There is no general introduction to this volume, each

chapter having its own. That on membership at first glance seems to be couched in terms similar to those of 1931:

> *Even at times of great difference of opinion, we have known a sense of living unity, because **we have recognised one another as followers of Jesus.** We are at different stages along the way. We use different language to speak of him and to express our discipleship. The insistent questioning of the seeker, the fire of the rebel, the reflective contribution of the more cautious thinker - all have a place amongst us. That does not always make life easy. But we have found that we have learned to listen to one another, to respect the sincerity of one another's opinions, to love and to care for one another. We are enabled to do this because God first loved us. The gospels tell us of the life and teaching of Jesus. **The light of Christ, a universal light and known inwardly, is our guide.** It is the grace of God which gives us the strength to follow. It is his forgiveness which restores us when we are oppressed by the sense of falling short. These things we know, not as glib phrases, but out of the depths of sometimes agonising experience.*
>
> *Membership, therefore, we see primarily **in terms of discipleship**, and so impose no clear-cut tests of doctrine or outward observance. Nevertheless those wishing to join the Society should realise **its Christian basis.***

The key phrases are those here emphasised in this quotation.

The 1931 'Spirit of Christ' has become the 'Light of Christ', and there is now no reference to the 'Lord and leader of all his disciples'. But in seeing membership 'primarily in terms of discipleship', they were explicit about whose disciples we Quakers were understood to be.

The Membership Review Committee

In 1976 Meeting for Sufferings set up a committee under this name. It submitted a report in 1983, accompanied by a discussion paper entitled 'The meaning of membership'. On its own recommendation, a new 'more broadly-based representative committee' was created. This reported to the 1989 Yearly Meeting, held residentially in Aberdeen. Proposals were submitted on 'acquisition of membership by adults'; 'the membership of children'; 'lapse of membership'; 'counting the Society's numerical strength'; and on 'dual membership'. Following clear indications that those present at Yearly Meeting were unable or unwilling to engage with these proposals, it was minuted that only those relating to the membership of children were accepted. These involved a clarification of the relevant portion of *Church Government* (1967). Thirteen years work, by about twenty Friends, was consigned to limbo.

At the end of our 'Past'

By 1993, more than half the adult membership of Britain Yearly Meeting had been accepted on the basis of the 1967 criteria. In its 1983 report the 1976 Membership Review Committee said 'it is clear that, in general, membership is now given more easily than formerly'. While the ethos remained broadly the same, the theological culture had not. For three hundred years Quakers could affirm that individually and corporately they were followers of 'the Inward Spirit of Christ'. Within a tenth of that time, it had become all but impossible to answer the question 'What do Quakers believe?'. And more and more individual members were finding it difficult to say what they themselves believed at whatever point they had reached on their spiritual journey.

THE PRESENT

1994 -2000

London Yearly Meeting changed its name in 1994 to Britain Yearly Meeting. The occasion for so doing was the adoption of *Quaker faith and practice: the book of Christian discipline of the Religious Society of Friends (Quakers) in Britain*[11]. Not only was this the first time it was in a single volume since 1883, but local meetings throughout the yearly meeting had been involved in the consideration of the draft Revision. The new book enshrines 'the present' for Britain Yearly Meeting, and it is to that we must turn, when considering our corporate approach to membership. But first we should stand back for a while, having looked so closely at one aspect of our own history.

Across the water

Just as it is all too easy for local meetings to become congregational in outlook, so we might continue here to focus upon the ways of our own yearly meeting. But some valuable perspective may be gained by drawing upon the experience and insights of others who share our history, and base their worship on silent waiting as we do here.

So let us view comparatively the way membership is approached by three long-established yearly meetings in the USA, and by ourselves:

New England[12]

Membership in the Religious Society of Friends, as a part of the Christian fellowship is both a privilege and a responsibility. Ideally, it is the outward sign of an inner experience of the living God and of unity with the other members of a living body. It implies a commitment to enter wholeheartedly into the spiritual and corporate activities of the Society and to assume responsibility for both service and support, as way opens. **Faith in God and an effort to follow the life and teachings of Jesus under the guidance and authority of the Light Within are the bases of our Quaker faith.** *The Society should reach out to and welcome into active membership all who find unity with the principles and the testimonies of Friends, as reflected in this book of* Faith and Practice.

New York[13]

MEMBERSHIP

Friends accept into active membership those whose declarations and ways of life manifest such unity with Friends' views and practices that they may be expected to enter fully into religious fellowship with the meeting. Part of the essential genius of the Society is the experience of growth through common worship and the loving acceptance of an individual into the group. It is an open fellowship that recognizes that of God in everyone.

Those inclined to join us should read carefully this entire book of Faith *and Practice and other Friends'* *literature so as to gain an understanding of the basis of the Quaker faith, mode of worship, and manner of transacting business. They should attend meetings for worship and for business for a sufficient period of time to become convinced that membership will nourish and enrich their continuing growth in the life of the Spirit. **They should be aware that this growth may entail changes in every aspect of their lives.***

Philadelphia[14]

*The Religious Society of Friends is **a community of faith based on experience of a transforming power named many ways: the Inner Light, the Spirit of Christ, the Guide, the Living God, the Divine Presence. Membership includes openness to an ongoing relationship with God and willingness to live one's life according to the leadings of the Spirit as affirmed by the community of faith**. For generations of Friends, membership has been an outward sign of an inward experience of Christ, the true light which gives light to everyone.* (John 1:9).

In Philadelphia Yearly Meeting, Friends gather to worship in stillness, waiting upon the Divine Presence. From this have come revelations of the love and guiding will of God, revelations inwardly experienced that may be shared in words with others present and expressed in attitude and action. Participation in this form of worship is intrinsic to membership, since ours is above all an experiential religion. Friends do not require acceptance of a creed as a test of membership, believing that no creedal statement can adequately describe spiritual reality.

*Membership establishes a commitment. It means that for each member the Religious Society of Friends provides the most promising home for spiritual enlightenment and growth. **It commits a person to the daily pursuit of truth after the manner of Friends and commits the Meeting to support the member in that pursuit.** Membership includes a willingness to live in spiritual unity with other members of the Religious Society of Friends.*

Members are expected to participate in communal worship, to share in the work and service of the Society, and to live in harmony with its basic beliefs and practices. Membership entails readiness to live as part of the monthly, quarterly, and yearly meeting.

And for ease of comparison, the relevant portions from our own *Quaker faith and practice* [11.01]:

Britain

*Membership is still **seen as a discipleship, a discipline within a broadly Christian perspective and our Quaker tradition, where the way we live is as important as the beliefs we affirm.***

*Like all discipleships, membership has its elements of commitment and responsibility, but it is also about joy and celebration. **Membership is a way of saying to the meeting that you feel at home, and in the right place. Membership is also a way of saying to the meeting, and to the world, that you accept at least the fundamental elements of being a Quaker:** the understanding of divine guidance, the manner of corporate worship and the ordering of the meeting's business, the practical expression of inward* *convictions and the equality of all before God. In asking to be admitted into the community of the meeting you are affirming what the meeting stands for and declaring your willingness to contribute to its life... There is a special responsibility to attend meetings for church affairs, for it is here the meeting enacts its faith. Membership also entails a financial commitment appropriate to a member's means, for without money neither the local meeting nor the wider structure can function.*

Membership does not require great moral or spiritual achievement, but it does require a sincerity of purpose and a commitment to Quaker values and practices. Membership is a spiritual discipline, a commitment to the well-being of one's spiritual home and not simply appearance on a membership roll.

[present emphasis in all quotations above]

The similarities and differences are apparent. All four yearly meetings make clear the need for commitment to the meeting and its affairs, expressed most strongly by New England and Philadelphia, least by Britain ('membership has its elements of commitment and responsibility'). The main difference lies between New York and Britain on the one hand, New England and Philadelphia on the other. Both the latter make explicit the need for inner personal experience ['...of the living God' (NE)]; ['...of a transforming power' (P)]. They both affirm unequivocally the member's need to seek and to follow the guidance of ['...the Light within' (NE)]; ['...the leadings of the Spirit, as affirmed by the community of faith' (P)]. New York removes the need for detail by its categorical requirement that an applicant has 'read carefully this entire book of *Faith and Practice*', and has also in other ways become familiar with 'the basis of the Quaker faith, mode of worship and manner of transacting business.' Britain Yearly Meeting has no such requirement, and when receiving her or his visitors, an applicant may well not have studied *Quaker Faith and Practice* at all.

It has to be said that in comparison with the statements from the three American yearly meetings, that from Britain is the least challenging. All four yearly meetings offer advice to those visiting an applicant for membership, New England and New York briefly, Britain and Philadelphia at greater length. The second pair also differ radically in their approach. Britain repeats parts of the introductory statement quoted above, and is discursive in style, while Philadelphia is explicit and practical:

> *The visit should take place in an atmosphere of openness and caring so that both the (clearness) committee members and the applicant feel comfortable in **exploring fundamental questions of religious belief and practice, and the responsibilities involved in membership in the Society.** Some questions the committee might ask are;*

>> *What are some milestones in your spiritual journey? How do you expect membership in the Meeting to help you in this journey?*

>> *What gifts do you believe you might bring to the Meeting community? In what ways would you like to share your time and talents with the Meeting?*

>> *How familiar are you with Friends' beliefs and practices? Are there some in particular which attracted you to Friends? Are there some you find puzzling or disturbing?*

Are you comfortable with a Society whose unity of spirit co-exists with a diversity of beliefs? Are you prepared to join a Society which includes people whose perspectives may differ from yours?

Have you weighed the Queries and Advices? Does their guidance speak to you?

How closely are you in harmony with Friends' testimonies? With Friends' work for social justice? Are you prepared to suffer (as Friends have done) if God calls you to take actions which are difficult, unpopular, or even contrary to the civil laws?

Do you understand the relationship between the monthly, quarterly and yearly meeting? Are you aware of and willing to meet our expectation of financial support for programs, services and facilities, at these three levels of our organisational structure?

On both sides of the Atlantic, some monthly meetings have felt it necessary to produce their own supplementary documents, for the use either of the applicant or the visitors. A recent example comes from Central Philadelphia Monthly Meeting: this is a comprehensive document on membership, intended for use by existing members as well as applicants and attenders; it was finally approved in late 1999 after two years work and consideration.

Though not being put forward as a model of its kind, it will serve to illustrate the relationship of such a local statement to the Discipline of the parent yearly meeting:

Central Philadelphia MM[15]

> Because God is infinite and we are finite we hold no expectation that we will come to a shared definition of that Mystery with which we strive to live in a covenant relationship. Indeed, we rejoice in the wide variety of ways in which we come to understand that Spirit. Some among us experience a loving and personal God, made manifest in the risen Christ; others' experience is of a Spirit which pervades and energizes the universe; still others among us are seeking a vital experience of a Presence that they cannot name, and still others continue a faithful journey through the desert seeking a God they believe to exist, but which they have not yet experienced. The vitality of our community is enhanced when we seek together for the revelation of the Spirit in our hearts and in our lives.
>
> We believe that by joining together in community we come closer to understanding both the individual and corporate roles we can play in witnessing to God's presence in the world. We are enriched when we speak with one another frankly and lovingly of our experience. We actively encourage each member's search for this understanding through our corporate religious practice, which has evolved over Friends' history of nearly 350 years, and continues to evolve as we gain new insights as a religious society.

This passage can be seen as emphasising the importance of membership in and of a religious community, that is capable of drawing upon a recognised and accepted diversity. It may be described as an 'unpacking' of the opening sentence of their yearly meeting's statement on the meaning of membership, already quoted.

Membership in Britain Yearly Meeting

Against this wider canvas we turn now to the present situation concerning membership, and its acquisition, in Britain Yearly Meeting.

The basis

The chapter on membership [11] in *Quaker faith and practice* starts with a two-page introductory section entitled 'The meaning of membership'. The opening paragraph in the 1967 revision is omitted [though set out in full, with approval, as the 'Conclusion' of the membership chapter (11.48)]. That omitted paragraph contained two statements making clear of whom we were seen to be disciples: '…we have known a sense of living unity, because we have recognised one another as *followers of Jesus*; and *'The light of Christ, a universal light and known inwardly, is our guide'*. These statements provided the essential antecedents for the use in the following paragraph of the term 'discipleship', which denotes the state of being 'one under leadership or pupillage' [*Oxford English Dictionary*].

The excised sentences are replaced by three short historical paragraphs, the first of which reads:

> *Today membership may not involve putting liberty, goods or life at risk but **the spiritual understanding of membership is, in essentials, the same as that which guided 'the Children of the Light'.** People still become Friends through 'convincement' and like early Friends they wrestle and rejoice with that experience.*
> *Membership is still seen as a discipleship, a discipline within a broadly Christian perspective and our Quaker tradition, where the way we live is as important as the beliefs we affirm.*

The first sentence makes an improbable assumption for which no evidence is provided; while the second sentence ignores a modern shift in the use of the term 'convincement'. As we have seen, 'early Friends' used the word to mean 'convicted' (of sin, of 'having missed the mark' in their lives). That is rarely the usage among British Quakers today. And then as noted above the next sentence is taken in isolation from the 1967 text, where it had read:

Membership, therefore, we see primarily in terms of discipleship, and so impose no clear-cut tests of doctrine or outward observance. Nevertheless those wishing to join the Society should realise *its Christian basis* 'and altered to read as above.' 'Christian basis' has become 'a broadly Christian perspective', while the concept of 'discipleship' is now given a central definitive role, despite being stripped of the essential antecedents located in the omitted paragraph. The 'fundamental elements of being a Quaker' are then set out as:

> *....the understanding of divine guidance, the manner of corporate worship and the ordering of the meeting's business, the practical expression of inward convictions, and the equality of all before God.*

Although these 'fundamental elements' cannot be said to make severe demands, Britain Yearly Meeting is clearly intended to be a religious body, if not a Christian one except in terms of personal behaviour. The commitment of membership is 'to Quaker values and practices', to the meeting and to the Society. A religious component is certainly implied, but its nature is not specified.

By application on behalf of a child

Birthright membership ceased at the end of 1959, along with what had been called 'Temporary membership' for children. The 1967 *Church Government* continued the 1931 provision of 'Admission on the application of parents'. In *Quaker faith and practice* under the heading 'Application on behalf of a child' we have:

> *Parents or those with parental responsibility or guardians who intend to bring up a child in accordance with the religious principles of the Society may apply for admission of that child into membership, while he or she is under the age of sixteen. [11.22]*

The monthly meeting must arrange for visitation, before reaching a decision as to admission into membership. (Here it ought to be acknowledged that **the meeting thereby accepts a pastoral responsibility for the child member**.) In 11.24 it is made quite clear that 'Membership acquired on parental application **constitutes full membership, and the member is under no obligation to confirm it on reaching a certain age**.' [present emphasis]. This may fairly be described as a modern variant of 'birthright membership' that is not automatically acquired, but has to be sought. It remains to be seen how many active Quakers it produces in the fullness of time.

On personal application

The section on membership in the 1931 *Church Government* included, for the first time, advice to those appointed as visitors to an applicant. This was done in the 1967 revision, and continues in *Quaker faith and practice*. Comparison of key passages from these three advices provides an illuminating perspective;

> *[1931]... the chief conditions to be looked for are that he is a humble learner in the school of Christ, that his face is set towards the light, and that he is able to find spiritual help and teaching in our Meetings for Worship, notwithstanding the absence of outward forms. If it seems clear that an experience of the reality and power of God is being manifested in him, he should be warmly welcomed into association with us. We believe that habitual dependence on the unseen Guide and Teacher, aided by the help that the Church can give, will lead him forward on the path of spiritual and practical Christianity.*

> *[1967] Moral and spiritual achievement in an applicant is not asked for; sincerity of purpose is. The chief conditions to be looked for are that he is a humble learner in the school of Christ; that his face is set towards the light; and that our way of worship helps him forward in his spiritual pilgrimage. Visitors may need to make it clear that the Society is essentially Christian in its inspiration, even though it asks for no specific affirmation of faith and understands Christianity primarily in terms of discipleship.*

> *[1994] (The visitors) should ensure that the applicant understands the nature of Quaker worship as a corporate waiting on God where inspiration and guidance may be received. The applicant should understand why we dispense with outward forms and should have considered seriously whether worship without them will be spiritually satisfying. Visitors will need to make it clear that the Society is essentially*

> *Christian in its inspiration, although it asks for no specific affirmation of faith and understands Christianity primarily in terms of discipleship ... Remember that moral and spiritual achievement is not what is required in an applicant; sincerity of purpose is.'*

In the 1994 version, 'humble learner in the school of Christ' and 'face set towards the light' are dropped, after surviving into the 1967 text, but perhaps the critical shift occurred in the latter, when the second and third sentences of the 1931 advice were dropped. The attention of the visitors is not directed, as it was in the 1931 version, to the applicant's *personal* experience of 'the reality and power of God', and of 'dependence on the unseen guide and teacher' in everyday life – not only in the course of Quaker worship. And 'sincerity of purpose' prompts the question 'What purpose?', to which we shall return later.

'Joint applications'

There are occasions when an application for membership may be made jointly by two Attenders, who may or may not be married. There is no provision for this in *Quaker faith and practice,* and for good reason. Each of the two persons concerned is an individual, with her or his independent and different life experiences. They will have travelled on different spiritual journeys, before and since meeting one another, and however much in harmony they may be about applying for membership, the basis of their applications must remain different. This necessary respect for them as individuals should be explained to them, and two pairs of visitors appointed.

Termination of membership

Membership can be terminated by resignation [11.36], or by the action of the monthly meeting in which membership is held [11.37 to 11.41]. *Quaker faith and practice* specifically enjoins overseers to recommend termination of membership 'once every effort has been made to follow up those who have drifted away from the meeting or have not been heard from for several years'. The phrase 'drifted away from the meeting' is open to a wide variety of interpretations.

A comparison between the number of members returned for the annual Tabular Statement, and the average number of members present at Meeting for Worship over a reasonable period, can serve as a starting point for questioning the extent to which termination is used in practice. The difference will usually be reduced when note is taken of members who take no active part in the worship or life of the meeting by reason of age or infirmity. Then a problem is raised by those members who never attend meeting, but continue making annual financial contributions: is that a satisfactory basis for remaining in membership? That leaves a residue of members who could attend meeting, but choose not to do so, and do not contribute financially or otherwise. Can these be identified as having 'drifted away from the meeting?' And if so, and follow-up efforts have been unavailing, should termination of their membership be recommended? And if not, why not? As a simple matter of Quaker integrity, should we be counting as members those whose commitment has lapsed?

That said, note should be taken of the words in *Quaker faith and practice* 11.41: 'Pleas for the continuance of formal membership on sentimental grounds should have no place in a religious society, but monthly meetings are reminded that many Friends go through periods, sometimes prolonged, when their association with the life of the meeting is tenuous.'

Membership practice in other Churches

How does our approach to membership compare with that of the mainstream Christian churches?

In the Church of England there is a very real sense in which all baptised persons are members, and are regarded as such. But confirmation is the general – though not universal – requirement before receiving communion, and is regarded as a way into fuller and more committed membership. To become involved in the 'business' of the Church, however, one has to be put on an electoral roll of the parish in which one lives, or the parish in which one worships: this is updated every five years, when fresh application must be made.

In the Methodist and United Reformed Churches, admission to 'church membership' goes along with a service of confirmation, for which both Churches have texts (though it seems that individual ministers can use their own). Only those who have been formally admitted to membership can vote, and play an active part in church government.

Membership of the Baptist Church comes through 'Believers' Baptism' as an adult, and is of a local Baptist church. This is governed by the Church Meeting, at which all members have a voice and a vote. The Church Meeting itself decides who may be admitted to membership, though faith in Jesus Christ is the sole condition required.

To become a member of the Roman Catholic Church involves a lengthy process – of instruction, confession, communion – and confirmation by the Bishop. There is no role for lay people in the decision-making processes of the Church, though some parishes have councils in which matters can be discussed.

A useful analysis is to be found in a 1988 report[16] of a British Council of Churches working party on 'the theology and practice of Christian initiation':

> *Membership is a portmanteau word, and different Christian traditions fill it with a varied amount of luggage. Necessary unpacking may be assisted by the introduction of the terms 'belonging' and 'incorporation'.*

> *Belonging denotes actual, experienced participation in the life of a Christian community. It also pertains to the community's perception and recognition of the individual's involvement in its life.* **To speak of informal belonging is to point towards the range of activities in which one may engage in the life of a community, of which one may not be a recognised 'member'.**

> *Incorporation' denotes the union of a person with Christ, and therefore and thereby with Christ's People … At the profoundest level, this is where the language of 'membership' belongs.* **A person becomes a 'member' within the one 'body'** *[present emphasis].*

The term 'informal belonging' could be used in a very positive way to describe the status of an active regular Attender in a Quaker meeting. 'Incorporation' might validly have described the position of Quakers in Britain until relatively recently. Since they ceased to be 'Christ's People', they have found it increasingly more difficult to define 'the one body' in religious terms.

Growing, shrinking, or static?

The total book-membership of Britain Yearly Meeting has been shrinking slowly for quite a long time – but not uniformly. At the end of 1998 there were *as many women as there had been thirty years earlier, but fourteen hundred fewer men*. In 1998 total adult book-membership fell below seventeen thousand, at the same time as the number of new members (on personal application) fell below three hundred – both for the first time. To replace losses by death, resignation and termination of membership by monthly meetings, all of which have on average remained stable, over five hundred new members are needed annually. *The shortfall averaged one hundred and sixty a year* during the late 1960s and early 1970s, and the 1990s have returned the same figure.

As would be expected, recruitment of new members varies across the yearly meeting area. Using the figures provided by the annual Tabular Statement, recruitment rates can be based either on the book-membership of the General Meeting, or upon the number of 'recognised Attenders' recorded at the beginning of the year. Both figures are inflated to an unknown extent, but that can be ignored for the present purpose, so long as one assumes the inflation to be about the same across the General Meetings. Using the book-membership as a basis invokes *size of General Meeting* as a possible element in comparison; using the number of attenders may relate recruitment of new members to previous outreach.

In 1998 the six General Meetings above the Yearly Meeting average on the book-membership basis were (in order) Devon & Cornwall; Scotland; Westmorland; Sussex &

Surrey; Hants, IOW & Channel Islands; Yorkshire. Of these, only Yorkshire was among the six largest GMs. Using the attender basis, the six top GMs were (in order) Devon & Cornwall; Sussex & Surrey; Yorkshire; Westmorland; Bedfordshire; Scotland. We are left asking why five GMs appear in both lists. During 1998 they accounted for 110 of the 297 new members across the yearly meeting – more than a third. The vigorous activities of Quaker Outreach in Yorkshire may well be a factor in that GM's relative success.

The 1998 new members were in a ratio of three to two, as between women and men, the same as that of the yearly meeting book-membership. Until recently there was a general expectation that more men than women would be appointed to serve as elders, while the reverse would be the case for overseers. This is no longer so: the proportion of women is significantly higher in *both* groups.

The overall situation cannot be described as satisfactory. The book-membership of the yearly meeting is falling slowly but steadily, because recruitment of new members regularly falls short of replacing losses by death, resignation and termination of membership. There is a serious shortage of men as compared with thirty years ago, a shortage which is not being reduced through the recruitment of new members.

It will be said that it is quality that matters, not quantity: we should not use numbers to 'look on the dark side', when there is still so much for which to be thankful and joyful in the life of our yearly meeting. Yes indeed: but this is a book about membership, not about our spiritual well-being – though the two are more closely related than is at times appreciated.

Overview

Adopting a two-pronged approach to our present membership situation, we have looked first at our current position on the meaning of membership, and its acquisition, against the background of the Disciplines of three yearly meetings in the USA, and (briefly) the practice of mainstream churches in Britain. Then we have reviewed the book-membership situation, and recent recruitment trends – both overall and across our General Meetings. A firm basis has thus been provided on which to consider our future course of action.

THE FUTURE

We have looked back into our history, and traced the story of Quaker identification from our beginnings. For ninety years there was no formal membership, but a process through which every newcomer had to pass before gaining acceptance by the local meeting. To at least the end of the seventeenth century, that process involved first a conviction of sin, of having 'missed the mark' in one's life: this was called 'convincement'. It was followed by the experience of 'conversion', change in one's personality through voluntary submission to what one discerned as being the purposes of God, the 'acceptance of God's dominion in one's life'. There is a sense in which this is never achieved, because it takes a lifetime. But one's fellow-Quakers would perceive the moment when that commitment had been made, when he or she 'knew a conversion of heart and soul'. At that point the meeting recognised the 'convinced person' as a Quaker, and accorded the right to 'sit in the business meeting'.

By the time formal membership was established in 1737, for reasons having little or nothing to do with individual belief and practice, the Society was entering a long period of inward-looking defensiveness, in which adherence to the 'testimonies' became the Quaker criterion. It came to rely for its continuance on the supply of replacements through the children of members, whose membership had by accident become in 1737 a birthright. For nearly a hundred years the intake of newcomers was in many areas minute or non-existent. And it was another hundred years before

– in 1931 – the need was recognised to address the topic of membership in the *Book of Discipline*, and to provide guidance to those appointed to visit an applicant for membership. The approach to the topic, and the wording of the guidance to visitors, were both modified in 1967, and remained unchanged until *Quaker faith and practice* was accepted by Yearly Meeting in 1994. With that event our 'present' commenced. In respect of membership, we know where we have come from and where we are today.

Membership under scrutiny

During the past year or so, individuals and groups have been posing questions about membership. Here are some of them:

> *What does membership mean to the individual today? What understanding of ourselves as a community does the current system embody? Is this still our corporate understanding? What possible ways forward can be identified?*

> *Is our commitment to God and to a way of life? or to a cosy club? What do our faith and commitment mean to us? What do we affirm / believe? Does it matter?*

> *What are the practical differences between being a member and being an attender? Does our current experience in the life of our meetings suggest that the time has come to look again at membership and attendership?*

This is perhaps the right point at which to assert our need for formal membership. In *Now we are Quakers*[17], I expressed it thus:

*'As a religious body without paid clergy, the Yearly Meeting cannot differ from any other corporate body: **responsibility for effective realisation of its avowed purposes is vested in those who have accepted a formal commitment to promote those purposes.** Only those – in a commercial cooperative society, a professional association, or a religious body – who are perceived publicly as committed members, can or should speak in the name of that society, association or body. However much any of us may wish, as some have said and written that they do, for an ideal situation in which "membership" could be abolished, so that anyone could say that he or she was "a Quaker" when they felt personally free to do so, it is not a practical proposition, and it will be in everyone's best interests – and that of our Quaker body – to recognise this'. [p.53]*

And here is a cogent passage from the 1999 Swarthmore Lecture[18]:

Membership is not an acquisition of rights but an acceptance of responsibilities, and is fundamentally a religious commitment.... Whereas an attender may be committed to only a fraction of the life and work of the Society – for example a local meeting for worship or Young Friends General Meeting – membership implies commitment to and at all levels. A member cannot regard any section of the Society as a group towards which they have no responsibility or commitment. No member should refer to the Yearly Meeting as 'them': it is fundamentally composed of 'us'. It is because membership matters that the process of application is and should be a serious and meaningful undertaking, not a mere formality.

I shall not attempt a systematic response to those exemplary questions, or elaborate on the passage just quoted – with which I am in full agreement. Challenged and illumined by the work and thought of others. I will try to evaluate our present situation, and then look forward in terms of perceived need for positive and effective action. Evaluation tends to be selective – and someone else might choose different targets from myself. For better or worse, here are my choices.

We need:

I   A careful evaluation of our current concept of membership, and of the process by which it is acquired, as laid down in Chapter 11 of our *Book of Christian discipline*

II A critical examination of our approach to the recruitment of new members.

I

MEMBERSHIP: CONCEPT AND ACQUISITION

A complete revision of *Quaker faith and practice* is unlikely to take place for at least 25 years. But the yearly meeting can and does alter portions of it from time to time, particularly in areas that deal with matters of church government. Membership is such an area.

But I have no intention of suggesting that we need another 'membership review committee': that way lies frustration and waste of resources, both human and of time. No – I think that the Yearly Meeting Agenda Committee is providing us (as I write) with a practical approach to consideration of the way in which we view membership. The first step is a session of Yearly Meeting 2000 entitled 'What it means to be a Quaker', with the intention of 'setting the agenda for work in local meetings towards consideration of more practical issues surrounding membership at residential Yearly Meeting 2001. Proposals for any consequent changes to membership procedures in our church government could be brought to a later Yearly Meeting'.

There are three elements in the *Quaker faith and practice* approach to membership and its acquisition:–

> *(a).*   *definition of membership, its essence and implications;*
> *(b).*   *advance advice to applicants;* and
> *(c).*   *guidance for the appointed visitors.*

As set out in chapter 11 of *Quaker faith and practice* they are all susceptible of improvement, despite the long and faithful work of the Revision Committee, and the less-than -detailed scrutiny in open sessions that was possible in the two parts of Yearly Meeting 1994. By way of illustrating what Friends could do at and after Yearly Meeting 2000, I will raise a few points – as examples, but nevertheless worthy I hope of serious consideration.

On (a): Definition of membership

(i)   We saw earlier how the term 'discipleship' was introduced in the 1967 revision of *Church Government*, and retained in 1994 [11.01 and 11.14], but now in isolation, because the preceding paragraph had been omitted. Without the antecedent reference to 'the teacher who is followed', it becomes an invalid notion – the use of the word disregards its actual meaning. *You cannot have discipleship without disciples and a teacher whom they follow*. You can, however, refer meaningfully to 'discipline' provided that you indicate whether it is required, freely chosen, or a mixture of both. The last sentence of the fourth paragraph of 11.01, with the words 'a discipleship' removed, would correctly imply an obligation accepted voluntarily by the act of seeking membership.

The term 'discipleship' also needs to be removed from the last sentence of 11.14.

(ii)   The preceding sentences of the fourth paragraph of 11.01 (starting with the words 'Today membership may not") require fresh attention, since they involve (as noted on page 24) questionable generalisations about the beliefs of British Quakers today.

(iii)   The phrase 'sincerity of purpose' is used twice [in 11.01 and 11.17]. *Without a stated aim it has no meaning*, and in this context it is important to establish what that aim is, especially when 'moral and spiritual achievement' have just been ruled out. As we saw earlier in this story of membership, sincerity of purpose was expected of 'convinced persons', and they *knew* what that purpose was: 'to come to know a *Conversion* in their hearts and souls.' Should that not still be the right aim in 2000 – *altering 'conversion' to 'change'? And if not, why not?*

(iv)   The extract from Edgar Dunstan [11.18] should be moved. It was a neat but to me wholly unacceptable way of recovering the phrase 'humble learner in the school of Christ' through the back door. It could surely be found a suitable place (as 10.35) at the end of the previous chapter.

On (b): Guidance to applicants

There are two points to be made about this (11.06-11.09). First, this guidance will not usually be seen in advance of the application, nor even of the visitation, unless the applicant has already studied this chapter of *Quaker faith and practice*. And second, it is inadequate anyway.

I have not been able to find an indication that its brevity was based on an assumption that monthly meetings would each set about amplifying it. In the event many have done so. I will reproduce here one of the earliest (again, not as a model):

> The visit of two experienced Friends with someone who wishes to join the Society marks a significant point in the process of becoming a member. The visitors come not to conduct an inquisition or to fill out a questionnaire, but to participate in a worshipful sharing of faith and experience. Their aims are: to ensure that you have no doubts or misunderstandings about membership of the Society, and to assure the Monthly Meeting that you have a basic understanding and experience of 'Quaker faith and practice'.
>
> There are no official rules as to how the visit should proceed, but here are the guidelines from which your visitors will have been invited to work.
>
> 1. Worship
>
> 2. Explaining the visit
>
> Your visitors will outline the role and plan of the visit and its possible outcomes, e.g. a fairly detailed report

to the Monthly Meeting, or a further visit, or perhaps a postponement if the application seems premature.

3. What has led you to apply?

They will encourage relevant biographical details, but will not wish to probe beyond what you are willing to impart. Please tell your visitors if there is anything you wish to have kept confidential. What they hope to hear from you is something about your religious or spiritual starting point, what experience you have had of various Quaker meetings and activities, and whether your wish to apply is based on any particular aspect of Quakerism.

4. Your understanding and experience of Quaker faith and practice.

None of the following aspects should be ignored or skirted around, but they need not be pursued in any particular order.

Worship after the manner of Friends.

Your visitors may ask: How do you cope with the silence? With the absence of outward forms and the elements of traditional church services? What is your understanding of spoken ministry and the gathered meeting?

Faith in the Quaker tradition.

Christian in roots and inspiration, universalist in scope and interpretation... Discipleship and testimony more important than any credal statement... 'Not a notion but a way'... How do you respond to the Quaker testimonies such as peace, equality, simplicity, integrity, and community?

Respect and tenderness.

Remember that 'What canst thou say?' applies to others as well as to oneself. If you describe yourself as Christian, can you seek and accept what is Christlike in those who do not? If not, can you accept and support those who hold to the distinctively Quaker strand of Christian tradition?

Church Government

Your visitors may ask about your understanding of meetings for church affairs, especially that of the Monthly Meeting. They may wish to talk about the role of clerks, elders and overseers, of the structure of the Society from local meeting level through to Britain Yearly Meeting and its links with the world-wide Quaker community.

The individual contribution.

Your visitors will remind you that the life of the Society depends upon its members' contributions of time, talent, and money. They will not seek specific commitments, but will leave you to consider your own level of response, according to circumstance, as and when the occasion arises.

5. Conclusion

Any questions? Any doubts? Agreement as to what happens next. (Report? Further visit?)

Closing worship

[Purley and Sutton MM 1995]

On (c): Guidance to visitors

This monthly meeting also produced a companion pamphlet to assist visitors. At least twenty of our seventy-three monthly meetings have taken similar initiatives in respect of one or both topics. There seems to be clear evidence that what is provided in *'Quaker faith and practice' is not perceived as meeting the needs of applicants or of visitors*, yet many meetings struggle on. Even if a decision were eventually taken to amplify the relevant sections in Quaker faith and practice, this need would persist for some years.

One temporary solution would be the early production as 'models' of two such pamphlets, by the Quaker Home Service Committee on Eldership and Oversight. I would expect full use would be made by that committee of the work already done by monthly and local meetings, rather than starting from scratch. It would be *essential for local meetings to hold stocks of the pamphlet offering guidance to possible applicants*, and for their availability to be made well-known. Supplies of the one offering advice to appointed visitors should be *held by the monthly meeting Clerk*, so that it could be sent out with her/his letter notifying the appointment as a visitor.

A practical alternative way of ensuring that every Attender writing a letter of application for membership had been provided with the available guidance would be to include it in the 'Attenders Pack' mentioned later. Pending the hoped-for amendment of references to 'discipleship' and 'sincerity of purpose' in 11.14 and 11.17 respectively, the pamphlet providing guidance for visitors can be mainly procedural. A current example of a monthly meeting initiative is available from South East Scotland Monthly Meeting:

The First and Subsequent Meetings and Meetings for Clearness

The visitors should contact the applicant as soon as possible and make clear the relaxed and informal nature of the meetings. They should stress that it is not an inquisition. Some applicants may feel somewhat apprehensive about the visit, so it is an occasion for sensitivity and tact.

The location can be wherever the applicant feels most comfortable – at his / her home, at the home of one of the visitors, at the Meeting House etc. The visit should be carried out in a spirit of worship, with a real sense of sharing with each other.

Before the meeting, visitors should refresh their memories of chapters 10 and 11 in Quaker faith and practice, *and jointly run through the list of items appended, remembering it is an 'aide memoire' and not a questionnaire. They should take copies of* Quaker faith and practice, Advices and Queries, Quaker News, The Friend *and the* Monthly Meeting Guide *along with them. Visitors should agree on how they will present their written report to Monthly Meeting.*

At the outset, the visitors should explain the purpose and form for the meeting. The discussion should start after a short meeting for worship and endeavour to explore the meaning of membership, the reasons for applying, personal circumstances, knowledge and experience of Quakers, and the responsibilities that accompany membership. Visitors should not feel that they need to cover all the ground at one meeting but should take as many meetings as they feel are necessary to ensure that the applicant is properly prepared for membership. Experience has shown that instead of beginning with questions it is often best that applicants should be encouraged to tell in their own way how they became attached to the Religious Society of Friends and why they wish to join.

Visitors should offer a meeting for clearness if the applicant would find it useful. If it is required, the visitors should contact either the suggested individuals or the Convenor of Overseers for arrangements to be made.

If the visitors feel that the Monthly Meeting will consider that the applicant is not ready for membership, this should be discussed during the visit.

In this example, the monthly meeting obviously felt that the advice to the visitors in *Quaker faith and practice* is insufficiently specific. The opportunity has been taken, without questioning the text, to expand and develop it in a positive way.

A note of caution

A firm advice issued by New York Yearly Meeting should find a place here:

Each meeting has a corporate personality of its own, so that is inevitable that there will be local coloration in the interpretation of membership requirements. This

should not be construed, however, as licence to impose
additional requirements for membership or to set aside
the guidelines in this Discipline. The receiving meeting
must be mindful of the fact that it acts not only in its
own behalf, but in the name of the Religious Society
of Friends in its entirety.

Meetings for clearness

In the example from South East Scotland MM above, the visitors were advised to 'offer a meeting for clearness if the applicant would find it useful'. Since few applicants are likely to know about such meetings, this advice would require the visitors to explain about them, before going on to ask whether the applicant 'would find it useful'. This directs our attention to the fact that all three American meetings quoted earlier use clearness committees in response to applications for membership. Although they are mentioned in 11.07, it appears to be only in relation to the consideration of 'important issues' *before the application is made*. There seems to be a good case for further examination of this potential approach to what we in Britain think of as the visitation. In her chapter on membership in *Searching the depths*[19], Helen Rowlands observes:

> *I think the concept of 'clearness' could be very*
> *appropriate, since it stresses the idea of questioning,*
> *of exploration, of seeking what God requires of us....*
> *Additionally it reinforces the idea of process, with the*
> *concept that more than one meeting of those involved*
> *might be helpful, rather than all hinging on one visit*
> *and a single decision by monthly meeting.*

Consideration of the question of 'preparedness' is postponed to the end of the next section, which deals with the recruitment of new members. I hope that my approach to the critical evaluation of the membership chapter in *Quaker faith and practice*, following five years of its use, will stimulate other Friends and meetings to do the same. The approach of others may well be different: what matters is that *we all take part in the process of evaluation and improvement.*

Younger Attenders

On a number of occasions Young Friends General Meeting has considered the difficulties that face younger Attenders who might wish to apply for membership. Most of these arise from occupational mobility, or from absence at university or other forms of higher education. Fresh consideration of this matter has recently commenced, and is focused in a Young Friends General Meeting minute as follows:

00/04 Membership: Identifying the Issues

There are practical difficulties with membership for some Friends, particularly those not based in a single place for long enough to feel part of a local meeting. Negative experiences of the bureaucracy involved in the membership process and sometimes of rigid attitudes from meetings have highlighted the issues of rejection and exclusion. It is important that we become members by convincement in order to show a formal commitment to a society we believe in, and not simply for convenience.

As a religious community, our membership is an expression of our faith. For some, this will be a process of trust, for others a careful even painful weighing-up. We ask Yearly Meeting to deeply consider the meaning and purpose of membership, whether the current system supports this purpose, and how greater flexibility could be built into whatever processes we have for membership, if any.

We thank all present for their open and heartfelt contributions to this ongoing process and encourage young Friends to attend Yearly Meeting.

As we noted in Part I of this book, membership has from the outset in 1737 been located in the monthly meeting. Without wishing (or even seeming) to pre-judge the outcomes of Yearly Meeting's review of the whole subject, I will venture a suggestion in response to the above Young Friends General Meeting minute.

When Young Friends General Meeting holds a meeting for worship for business, all those present during the weekend or other conference in which it takes place are encouraged to attend. Some of those will be in membership of the Society. Could regulations be drawn up that would enable those members to constitute a 'monthly meeting' for the purpose of dealing with membership matters? That 'monthly meeting' would need a clerk and some overseers. On receipt of an application a clearness group would be appointed, to meet with the applicant and to report to a later meeting.

Those becoming members in this way would at some point need to seek transfer of membership to that monthly meeting, of which the meeting they usually attended was a part.

II

RECRUITMENT OF NEW MEMBERS

We turn now to the facts of our current situation.

On average Britain Yearly Meeting needs to welcome about five hundred and twenty new members a year, simply to replace losses by death, resignation, and terminations by monthly meetings. On average it falls short of this by about one hundred and sixty a year. Are we concerned about this, and if so what should we do about it?

I am concerned about it – enough to examine our current approach to recruitment, and then to put forward for discussion some thoughts on ways to improve it. There are two clear stages in the recruitment of new members. In the first stage, we have to attract the interest of those who have never experienced a Quaker meeting for worship, sufficiently to persuade them to sample one. That we correctly call 'outreach', but we have to extend the use of this term to include a necessary transition towards frequent or even regular participation, at which point we think of the person as an 'Attender'. The second stage we know to involve the passage of time, learning about our heritage and our current faith and practice, and then the attender's realisation that he or she may feel ready to make a commitment, to 'throw in their lot with us'. The support needed during that second stage I will call 'inreach'. Let us examine our current position and practice in respect of each of these stages.

Outreach

In the latter half of the seventeenth century, Quakers proselytised and evangelised actively, and drew many thousands to their local meetings. As we have seen, in many parts of Britain that activity faded away for more than a hundred years. Today many Friends are quick to assert that we do not proselytise, not always using that word correctly. It means 'to try to draw people away from their present religious affiliation'. These days we do not proselytise, nor should we in the light of our corporate commitment to positive inter-church and inter-faith relations. But we *should evangelise* –'proclaim our good news' – as vigorously as we can. Again mistaking the meaning, or just not liking the implication of a need for 'evangelical zeal', British Quakers prefer to talk about 'outreach'.

As we have noted, that is the appropriate term for what is done in an organised way to let 'people out there' hear about Quakers, and to encourage them to 'give us a try'. In 1998 the Outreach section of Quaker Home Service sent out nearly fifteen hundred 'enquirers packs' to those responding to our media publicity; this resulted in a large correspondence. Practical and personal support was given to the outreach efforts of many local meetings. That (and other) remarkable activity on the part of a very small team certainly accounts for some of those who have found themselves in a Quaker meeting for the first time.

There is however evidence that more than a third of fairly regular attenders had been in previous contact with a Quaker or an attender at a Quaker meeting, and had as a result tried it for themselves. I think of that as 'personal outreach', and value it highly. Then there are those from Quaker families – another fifth of the total – who had continued or recommenced attendance at a Quaker meeting. And of course some people come of their own accord, through reading or out of curiosity or a sense of need. Whatever the route, if they keep on coming, even if irregularly, they have been 'reached'.

At the end of 1998 the seventy-three monthly meetings of Britain Yearly Meeting reported a total of over nine thousand Attenders. Here I must emphasise that *there is no way of knowing how closely those responsible in each meeting for counting their attenders adhered to the definition in* Quaker faith and practice. '... one who, not being a member, frequently attends a specific meeting for worship'. 'Frequently' is an imprecise and very flexible term: in sharp contrast, the old term 'habitual attender' has much to commend it.

Our investment in outreach, through the organised energetic work of a small professional staff in Quaker Home Service, over many years; the regional activities of such bodies as Quaker Outreach in Yorkshire; and the varied efforts of local meetings, have clearly paid off. In spite of an average turn-over in attenders of ten to twelve per cent a year, total numbers have been maintained at a high level. We must conclude that *outreach in all its forms is successful across the yearly meeting as a whole.* At the local meeting level that is not always the case.

Inreach

Moving on to the second stage, involving the significant transition from Attender to Member, we encounter a very different situation.

The yearly meeting recruitment rate, defined as 'the percentage of those listed as attenders at the end of the previous year who, twelve months later, had become members', has fallen fairly steadily from a peak of over seven per cent in 1984 to the 1998 figure of just over three per cent. Even if one reduces the numbers of 'listed attenders' by an arbitrary one-third, to allow for 'inflation' at monthly meeting level, the recruitment rates only move up to eleven and five per cent respectively.

Enough of statistics. They have served to make clear where we are failing. We attract and keep large numbers of attenders, but are unable to bring more than a tiny handful to seek membership. *Successful outreach is not followed by successful inreach*, in spite of the active support given to regional and local efforts by the Quaker Home Service Outreach section. It is time to seek the reasons for this failure, keeping well to the front of our minds that, for all practical purposes, *new members can come only from our active Attenders*.

The first reason is rooted in the culture of society at large. For twenty years at least, our culture has more and more rejected personal commitment, to any person or to any organisation. You enter into a commitment if it is the only way to get what you want. Having recognised that as being for many attenders an important element in their attitude to membership, and one that we must quietly strive to overcome, let us move on in search of less 'global' factors.

The report of the first Membership Review Committee[20] contained the following passage:

> *We have encountered many Attenders who share actively in our life and work, but who will not apply*

for membership. Their reasons vary: some will not join any sect or denomination for ecumenical reasons; some think that a truly Christian body should be open-ended; some 'cannot live up to our standards', while others think that we don't live up to them; some don't want to become involved in our activities, or disapprove of our testimonies.

That summary of 'reasons why not', while useful in itself, also draws attention to what is missing. For example, seventy attenders with whom discussions were held (in their own homes) saw Quakers as

- poor communicators, at a personal face-to-face level, on matters of faith and experience.

- Many of them saw us as tending to be diffident, and as seekers ourselves rather than as finders.

- They expressed need for more teaching, in a systematic way and on a regular basis.

- Many referred to Quakers as being 'busy', both with their Quaker duties and more generally. For some attenders *this was seen as an obstacle to their own possible* application for membership, since 'commitment' was often mentioned as a key concept in that context.

- They also spoke of the shortcomings at local-meeting level of basic information needed by attenders, especially if they were beginning to think about applying for membership.

The report[21] of a survey of all those becoming members across the yearly meeting during 1992 included the fact that *nearly half the two hundred responding new members said that they had received no encouragement to apply for membership – from anybody.*

* * *

The ball is in our court, Friends. What are the key questions? I offer the following for consideration, together with my immediate comments:

Towards a practical strategy

1. *Are preparative and monthly meeting nominations committees experiencing greater difficulty in identifying seasoned Friends, for service as clerks, elders, overseers and treasurers? Is that becoming the case in your meeting?*

I lack the information to generalise about 'the difficulties of PM and MM nominations committees', but would hope that Quaker Home Service Central Committee or the Committee on Eldership and Oversight are in a position to do so. The latter is already working on this subject of membership, and must have a key coordinating role in the work that needs to be done in and by our meetings, following Yearly Meeting 2000.

On the basis of what I have read, and heard informally, in recent months, I think that we have become generally aware of a growing lack of seasoned Friends. Here is one example. A local meeting has a book-membership of about 150, nearly thirty of whom live outside the area, and a further twenty are precluded by age or infirmity from taking on an active role. Of the remainder, it is estimated that about two-thirds attend meeting for worship fairly frequently, somewhat over half that number on any particular Sunday. Attenders are approached for service to the meeting, in roles that do not involve being asked 'to speak on behalf of Quakers', or (within the meeting) the acceptance of personal responsibility. They are not asked to serve as clerks, elders or overseers. This is felt and perceived to be a vigorous meeting.

When nominations were being sought by its monthly meeting at the start of the new triennium, eleven Friends in that meeting were approached for nomination as elders, of whom six accepted. Seventeen out of the twenty-four Friends approached for service as overseers declined. Of the seven accepting, one had just had a three-year break after a previous nine years continuous service. To meet the needs of the meeting, twelve elders and at least the same number of overseers, preferably more, were sought. Most of those declining nomination had already given service, and several referred to lack of what I have elsewhere[22] described as 'disposable time'. Not one of them could be thought of as shirking their responsibilities as members.

I am reliably informed that the situation just described, while not necessarily typical is 'not all that unusual'. One Friend, during discussion in a consultation at Woodbrooke, expressed the problem succinctly: 'We have a labour shortage'. Whether wholly or partly in response to such shortage, more than seventy local meetings are not served by elders and overseers appointed by their monthly meeting. Members worshipping in the local meeting endeavour instead to share responsibility for pastoral care among themselves. Monthly meetings are enjoined [*Quaker faith and practice* 12.15] 'to have a particular care' for such meetings. I do not know the extent to which such essential oversight is being carried out.

2. Do we need more members to replace our losses, and to be invigorated as a yearly meeting?

Personally I am absolutely certain that we need many more members, not just to keep our structures functional, but gradually and steadily to rejuvenate the make-up of our active membership. That we are experiencing considerable ongoing difficulty reflects not only the rapidly-changing culture in which we live, but also *a serious lack of the visible and audible evidence of that first-hand spiritual experience, upon which a religious body without creed or clergy must depend for its validity.* Yes: we must witness through our lives, but also – if we are in a condition to do so – through our personal testimonies to the guiding and empowering action of the Spirit within them. Our active Attenders are not sheep – but many do 'look up and are not fed'.

3. Do we recognise that outreach continues to be **generally** *successful in providing and maintaining the only source from which new members can come?*

Outreach does continue overall to be very successful, reflecting both the organised central work, and what happens in many local meetings. Arrival in the meeting through personal contact may often turn 'enquirer' into 'attender' because, as the latter have reported, we Quakers are usually 'friendly, accepting and tolerant'. But there are meetings with few or no regular attenders, sometimes but not always due to their small size or geographical location. Those meeting in one another's homes, in mainly rural areas, face a special difficulty.

4. Should our limited central outreach resources now be **focused** *on a sensitive offering of assistance to those monthly* *meetings that have the **lowest** number of regular attenders, relative to their number of active members?*

Given limited resources, there is I think a strong case for *a more focused approach to organised outreach measures,* whether centrally, regionally or locally executed. Areas or meetings which seem unable to attract visitors and enquirers, and then to give them reason to stay as attenders, should be approached sensitively with offers of appropriate and acceptable help. When such an offer has been accepted and implemented, *supportive follow-up would be essential*: this must not be a modern version of the old one-off 'mission'.

Our greatest weakness today is the near-absence of a teaching ministry, provided in the 17th and 18th centuries by the 'travelling ministers'. We cannot turn back the clock, but we can be inventive and resourceful in devising a modern equivalent.

*5. Is your meeting ready to look critically at the ways in which it might **better inform, nurture and encourage its attenders?***

and

*6. Has the time come to be **more systematic in our provision** of opportunities for regular attenders to learn about our Quaker heritage, faith and practice?*

During the last nine years I have been among those with a particular concern about our many Attenders. Through participation in the work of Quaker Outreach in Yorkshire, and invited opportunities to visit meetings in various parts of Britain, I became convinced that we have a serious problem, located in our local meetings – and that it needs urgently to be addressed. That problem is clearly identified by the wording of those two related questions. I will return to it later in this section.

7. Should additional **special resources be sought,** *to enable sustained assistance to be offered to those meetings with* **adequate numbers of regular attenders,** *but the* **lowest** *annual membership recruitment rates?*

My answer is an emphatic 'Yes!' even though I fully realise that such 'special resources' are unlikely to be available within normal budgets, given the current limitations of Britain Yearly Meeting's Central Fund. So a carefully worked-out project needs to be designed, and placed before the appropriate committee for consideration. Once it is approved as being 'in right ordering', efforts should be made to obtain the necessary external funding from one or more trusts and individuals.

TAKING MEMBERSHIP SERIOUSLY

We ordinary Friends in many of our local meetings are challenged by the current situation and trends. The challenge is to change both our attitudes and our behaviour. I have said 'in *many* of our local meetings' because I am sensitive to the very real difficulties faced by some of our meetings, despite positive attitudes and active behaviour in this domain. And I am also aware that many meetings have already addressed some of these matters, in some cases taking fresh action.

On attitudes

1. Both outreach and inreach are primarily *our* responsibility, *not* mainly that of a small section in an under-

funded central department of our yearly meeting. Replacement of losses and the introduction of new life in our membership is *our* job, and demands from us a high priority. That responsibility rests upon *each one of us*: it should not be laid solely upon elders or a relevant small committee.

2. We should perceive *every active regular Attender* as a potential member, unless there are positive reasons not to do so. This means abandoning the widespread shibboleth about 'not pressing' anyone: attenders are more likely to be hurt by feeling ignored than by being pressed. Many of them have said so. There is a real difference between 'pressing' and encouraging, stimulating – even occasionally challenging. Most Attenders respond to all three of these approaches, and it is not difficult to spot those shy, reserved ones who need a sensitive, gradual approach.

These observations are intended as challenges to feeling comfortable, enjoying 'the even tenor of our ways'. You and your meeting are simply being asked to have a fresh look at your attitudes in this urgent matter. You are **not** being asked to feel guilty – or to line up your excuses for inaction!

On behaviour

My use of this term has no moral undertones: it serves to cover all our actions, everything that we say and do, individually and corporately.

1. In the Yorkshire Attenders Survey[23] the question was posed: 'Since you began to attend, how have you found out about Quakers and their history and beliefs?' The largest single item, accounting for more than a quarter of the

responses, was 'reading Quaker literature'. In a recent article[24] on meeting libraries, Peggy Heeks confirmed my own impression that there are many meetings in which the 'library' consists of a few shelves of shabby and outdated books. Constructively, she suggests getting 'a couple of Friends from another meeting to "speak truth to you in love", with coffee and cakes thrown in'. She also stresses the importance of the library having a budget each year, and of a PM policy to go with it. I cannot recommend her article too highly: it is full of practical wisdom, so by permission it is reproduced here as an *Appendix*.

So perhaps the very first thing your meeting needs to do for your Attenders is to *re-value the importance of your library*.

2. There is another way in which you can meet the need for Quaker literature *You can have it available for sale*. Only a handful of our nearly four hundred local meetings do so, I can appeal to the majority. Let me ask you to imagine that you are an Attender in a Quaker meeting, and that you are in conversation with one of its friendly members over coffee. You express interest in reading about the history of Quakers here in Britain, and on learning that there is a short and inexpensive book available, you say you would like to get a copy.

Now I must ask you a question: 'How would you – if you were that Attender – react to being told to "Get in touch with the Quaker Bookshop at Friends House in London, to order a copy. They will tell you the cost, including packing and postage". "Would you bother?" Maybe.

If your meeting seriously wants to serve, stimulate and encourage its Attenders, it should arrange with the Bookshop to have, for sale in the meeting-house, two or three copies of each of the less expensive Quaker books, on the subjects in which Attenders are most likely to be interested. We know what these are, because Attenders have told us what they want.

The main criticism was about the inaccessibility (or lack of ready availability) of the information that an attender might welcome or need. Specific matters included the whole process of application for membership; Quaker structures and processes; the 'special terms' and all the initials and acronyms; and the fact that attendance is possible on request at meetings for worship for business.

3. Some meetings have made up an 'enquirers pack', which is offered free to first-time visitors, and to people using the meeting house during the week. A different pack is needed for regular Attenders. More than a quarter of the new members already quoted had begun to think about the possibility of membership by the end of their first year, a further quarter during their second year. That seems to make a good case for presenting the Attenders pack at or about the one-year point, along with a friendly enquiry as to whether he or she has been getting adequate support and encouragement. Invitations to tea or a meal are less frequent these days, and often valued all the more.

4. Most local and regional activity takes the form of isolated one-day events. Some years ago, Quaker Outreach in Yorkshire perceived the need to run such events separately for enquirers and newcomers on the one hand, and for Attenders on the other. Their needs are different. Useful as they are, however, two defects are in-built. First, participation depends on a variable mix of interest, availability of free time, and travel arrangements and cost. And second, the range of topics is of necessity limited. But

the greatest weakness is the *lack of follow-up back in the Attender's meeting.*

5. When Attenders were asked 'How could the meeting/its members have assisted the process of 'finding-out'?', more than half the responses were accounted for by two items. These were 'by offering fairly frequent short courses on Quaker toplcs' and 'more regular opportunities for informal learning'. This draws attention to the general lack of what might be called a systematic approach – which would certainly be possible in our middle-sized and larger meetings.

One such produced its own version of a 'fairly frequent short course', loosely based on one developed in an American meeting. This British one consisted of three topics: Quaker history; Quaker structures; and Quaker faith and practice. Sessions held on Sundays after a picnic lunch (a fortnight apart) were introduced and led by three members of the meeting. Attendance varied, but this was catered for by two repeats of the complete course, some months apart. This system allowed an individual Attender, who was obliged to miss one or more of the topics, the chance to 'pick them up' the next or subsequent time around. By keeping a record of those present on each occasion, it was possible to establish that most of the meeting's active Attenders had completed the 'course'. It was then discontinued for a year before being offered again. Several meetings have taken similar initiatives, notably Exeter which for several years made use of the study pack *You and the Quaker tradition.* [25]

Preparedness

Most of what has been set out above is simply illustrative of active inreach measures; it is far from being exhaustive. The common objective is to ensure that every active Attender is provided with the information, stimulation, encouragement and support, that will enable her or him to feel more fully 'at home' among us than is possible solely through the Sunday morning Meeting for Worship, and our social activities. The aim is to reach a condition of what we saw described as 'informal belonging'.

Any Attender who has taken full advantage of what has been made available, and has reached that condition, could be described as 'prepared' for membership, if feeling ready to apply. Here I must emphasise that *the primary aim of all such inreach is to care for and nurture each individual*, not to recruit another member. Our subsidiary aim is to enable those who do reach the point of seeking membership to be well-prepared for that step.

The shortcomings of our yearly meeting's application process are now apparent. There is no systematic provision for ascertaining the extent of 'preparedness' *before the application has been made*. This could be remedied as follows:

In the 'Advice to the applicant' in *Quaker faith and practice* 11.07, delete the sentence 'Letters of application ... a plain request', and amend the following sentences to read

> *'Before writing you should approach one of the elders or overseers about your intention. A clearness group will be set up on behalf of the monthly meeting,*

*including one or more members of the
local meeting nominated by yourself. This
group will be happy to discuss any
questions or thoughts you may have about
membership, and to explore your
familiarity with our Quaker heritage, faith
and practice.'*

At this point, we have a choice: to carry on with our present
practice of appointing two visitors, on receipt by the Clerk
of the written application; *or* to dispense with this
appointment by designating the clearness group as the
body to report to monthly meeting. The latter course has
much to commend it. It would involve the applicant fully
from the outset, and remove what for some is daunting –
the meeting with the two visitors. Monthly meeting would
be assured that the applicant was reasonably well prepared
for membership, since the clearness group would have
delayed reporting had that not been the case. A decision to
delay would have involved the applicant, and so any possible
hurt would be avoided. This process would demonstrate
the kind of 'openness' to which we are corporately
committed.

One monthly meeting has been developing a scheme of
preparation, that involves an approach to regular Attenders
at an early stage. A short informative booklet ['Notes for
Attenders and Friends[26]] is freely available in the meeting,
which is drawn to the attention of any newcomer who has
attended fairly regularly for at least a year. If it seems that
there is possible interest in applying for membership at
some point, the attender is encouraged to explore the
Quaker heritage and current practice with an overseer or
elder in the meeting that he or she usually attends. To
broaden the perspective, a member of a panel of 'Supporting

Friends', set up by the monthly meeting, will be invited to join in this process.

At this point the scheme departs from the application procedures laid down in *Quaker faith and practice* 11.12. No visitors are appointed, and the application is in effect prepared jointly by the attender and the two 'nurturing Friends'. The monthly meeting will be assured that the applicant is sufficiently well prepared. While it then exercises its judgment in the usual way, there is an expectation of acceptance. Only if there is a doubt will the monthly meeting set up a clearance group to take the process further before a decision is made.

The word 'should' in the quotation from *Quaker faith and practice* 11.12 is prescriptive, not merely advisory. While the process of preparation must be warmly welcomed, the independence of a visitors' report is needed, unless and until the yearly meeting decides to replace it, perhaps along the lines of the suggestion above, concerning the use of clearness groups.

An essential objective

Commitment is not just 'an element' of membership, in the throwaway phrase of *Quaker faith and practice* 11.01: it is *central* to it, along with conviction. Both are essential for the spiritual health of a faith community. We started with a recognition that commitment is very difficult to elicit in our present culture. That alone may account for most of our regular Attenders continuing as such, in many cases for years. But it is *not* the only cause: there are at least two others. We do not nurture, encourage or challenge them enough; and we often fail the crucial test of living testimony.

Persevering Attenders remain unconvinced because so many Quakers seem unconvinced themselves– or cannot find the words with which to explain *what it is of which they are convinced.*

In sum: we need a considerably greater inflow of new members. The only place from which these can be drawn is our large following of active Attenders. In this chapter we have considered ways in which our inreach to them can be significantly improved, as well as ways in which their transition to membership could be made positively more attractive. And we have evidence of a failure on our part to provide *the visible and audible evidence of that first-hand spiritual experience, upon which a religious body without creed or clergy must depend for its validity.*

The very act of applying for membership should be evidence that the man or woman has accepted an inward call to change. A significant stage has been reached, the possibility of continuing growth lies ahead. And growth implies change.

But we members, we Quakers are ourselves challenged. In Penn's words:

> 'They were changed men themselves before
> they set about to change others.'

Yes: but you and I know full well that we cannot suddenly become changed men and women, even in response to the need of others. But we *can* live adventurously – and ask God to show us how to grow. As we do so, and share that experience, others will feel drawn to join us. Commitment will evoke commitment, and our community will be strengthened, both in numbers and in depth.

Marketing the Meeting's library[24]

Meeting libraries are amongst our most precious assets and resources. How can we better ensure that they are meeting the needs of members, attenders and enquirers?

Surveys regularly show the PM library is a major factor in encouraging learning and strengthening spiritual life. Quaker Home Service's recent findings echo my own, published in 1998.

Being told that the library is 'really beneficial' heartens us, comfortingly confirms our view of how things should be. It takes us back to Milton's reassurance that 'a good book is the precious life-blood of a master spirit'.

Probe into the statistics, though, and there are grounds for unease. Although borrowing from the Meeting's library is acknowledged as 'a good thing', my study showed only about 50 per cent of members and attenders actually doing so, with just 20 per cent regular users. This picture was corroborated in a series of conferences on 'Libraries in the life of our Meetings', held a few months ago. The main problem raised was under-use of the library's resources.

In the face of this gap between belief and reality, I have encouraged PM librarians to ask themselves the classic question for any organisation: 'What business are we in?' The obvious next question is: 'How is the business doing?', and here the traditional 'four Ps' of marketing can help: 'product', 'place', 'price', 'promotion'. Examination of our

Quaker libraries under these headings may suggest ways of making them more effective.

Product: Our product is something beyond the books, the tapes, the videos that make up the library's stock. These are important as the means to the end. That end was defined variously at the regional conferences, showing the riches a library can offer: information for enquirers; help for pastoral care; material for study groups; challenge for established Friends; nurture for those in trouble; inspiration for life's journey.

Such an exercise is essential, not just for the library committee, but for the whole Meeting. Until a Meeting works out its hopes from the library, it's impossible to decide what stock to buy.

Place: What message does the physical environment of your library convey? I once heard a public library described as 'the dingiest tome tomb in the area' and the same could be said of some of our PM libraries. Shabby books and outdated books aren't going to provide the challenge and inspiration mentioned among library aims.

After a while one loses the ability to look at the library as a newcomer would, so it's helpful to get a few people not closely associated with the library to assess its appearance. This is the point to remember that Monthly Meetings have a library responsibility (*Quaker faith & practice* 13.40), so you could invite a couple of Friends from another PM to 'speak truth to you in love' - with coffee and cakes thrown in.

Library intervisitation could be an enjoyable exercise. It's amazing what creative ideas can emerge in a group trying a bit of lateral thinking. 'Location, location, location' applies as much to a library as to a house. It may be better to trade in a large inaccessible room for a smaller central space.

Once the library room or area is attractive and welcoming, it's time to go through the stock and throw out books that are in poor condition or irrelevant to the Meeting's needs: they just depress the whole atmosphere.

Price: Price is of obvious importance in marketing a business, but what has it to do with Meeting house libraries? First, this heading is a reminder that the library needs an annual budget, set by the PM. It's important that the Meeting should decide how much of its income to allocate to library purposes. It may sound great to be told 'Oh, spend what you think is reasonable' but, in practice, you can't plan spending wisely without a budget. Price comes into consideration in another way in some PM libraries, where stock is chosen largely on grounds of cost. 'We have a policy of never buying anything costing more than £5.99'. Is that a good policy? Shouldn't we be deciding what kind of stock is needed, what subjects should be covered, rather than making price the deciding factor?

Promotion: There's no one way of promoting the library. A promotion strategy should allow for a range of approaches. A library with clear signs, displays, posters, comfortable chairs and good lighting will attract attention. Reviews of two or three books in each newsletter arouse interest, especially if they involve a range of Friends, not just the librarian.

People are better promoters of books than print, so it's worth thinking how you can introduce this personal element, perhaps by showing new books after Meeting, using book groups or personal recommendation. Consider targeted promotion to overseers, elders, children's committee. Sometimes just the large number of books on the shelves may be a deterrent, so overcome this by themed displays or a 'Books of the month' feature.

There are two others Ps I would add to the traditional marketing quartet. The first is policy. Without a policy, agreed by PM, it's hard to judge whether the library is doing its job. The second is partnership. Some Meetings have a library committee, while in others the librarian operates alone. Either way, the library can seem quite unconnected with other PM structures, isolated and so overlooked. Part of promoting the library lies in forging partnerships with other groups, and especially with elders whose responsibilities for learning are so close to those of the library.

• Peggy Heeks is a member of Witney Monthly Meeting.

[Printed by kind permission of Peggy Heeks and the Editor of The Friend*]*

In 'Letters to the Editor' of *The Friend*, 17.iii.00:

'Moira Field's gentle rebuke of 10 March encourages me to add to my article. Shabby books *do* depress the whole library atmosphere, but there are alternatives to throwing them away; get them rebound, repaired, or put them in a reserve stock. Just as stock needs to be added regularly, so it needs regular review.

I would certainly suggest we judge books on grounds of relevance rather than age. There should always be space for Quaker classics.'

REFERENCES

1. *Quaker faith and practice, 27 ,25*

2. *Book of extracts: Christian and brotherly advices given forth from time to time by the Yearly Meeting in London* . [1782]

3. **Robert BARCLAY,** *An apology for the true Christian divinity* 1678.

4. **Richard T. VANN,** *The social development of English Quakerism 1655-1755.* Cambridge, Mass. Harvard University Press 1969.

5. **John PUNSHON,** *Portrait in grey: a short history of the Quakers.* London: Quaker Home Service 1984.

6. **W.C.BRAITHWAITE,** *The second period of Quakerism.* London: Macmillan 1921.

7. See (5) above

8. See (4) above

9. **John S.ROWNTREE,** *Quakerism past and present.* London: Smith Elder 1859.

10. *Church Government* (Pt.3 of *Christian discipline in the Religious Society of Friends in Great Britain*) 1931.

11. *Quaker faith and practice: the book of Christian discipline of the Yearly Meeting of the Religious Society of Friends (Quakers) in Britain.* London: Quaker Home Service 1995.

12. *Faith and practice of New England Yearly Meeting of Friends.* 1986.

13. *Faith and practice: the Book of Discipline of New York Yearly Meeting of the Religious Society of Friends.* 1998.

14. *Faith and practice: a Book of Christian discipline of Philadelphia Yearly Meeting of the Religious Society of Friends.* 1997.

15. *On being a member.* Central Philadelphia Monthly Meeting. 1999.

16. *Christian initiation and church membership.* London: The British Council of Churches 1988.

17. **Alastair HERON,** *Now we are Quakers: the experience and views of new members.* York: Quaker Outreach in Yorkshire 1994.

18. **Alex WILDWOOD,** *A faith to call our own.* London: Quaker Home Service 1999.

19. **Helen ROWLANDS.** 'The meaning of membership', in *Searching the depths: essays on being a Quaker today* (Harvey Gillman & Alastair Heron, Eds.). Quaker Home Service 1998.

20. *Report of the Membership Review Committee* 1983.

21. (See (17 above)

22. **Alastair HERON,** *Our Quaker identity: religious society – or friendly society?* Kelso: Curlew Productions 1999

23. **Alastair HERON**, *Caring–conviction–commitment: dilemmas of Quaker membership today* . Quaker Home Service and Woodbrooke College 1992.

24. **Peggy HEEKS**, 'Marketing the Meeting's library'. *The Friend* , 18 February, 2000 pp 7-8.

25. **Harvey GILMAN**, *You and the Quaker tradition: a pack for Attenders.* Quaker Home Service and Woodbrooke College. London. 1994.

26. *Notes for Attenders and Friends.* Nottinghamshire and Derbyshire Monthly Meeting. 1999.

Publications in print, by the same author

Obtainable from:
Quaker Bookshop, Friends House, Euston Rd, London NW1 2BJ
Caring, conviction, commitment: dilemmas of Quaker membership today (83 pp) Quaker Home Service and Woodbrooke College 1992. Based on a survey of the experiences and views of 459 Attenders across Yorkshire General Meeting

Gifts and ministries [2nd (revised) edition] (22 pp). Quaker Home Service 1993. A discussion paper on eldership.

Now we are Quakers: the experience and views of new members (64 pp). Quaker Outreach in Yorkshire 1994. The experiences and views of 200 men and women, across the whole yearly meeting, who became Members during the year 1992.

QuakerSpeak: first aid for newcomers [2nd (revised) edition] (66 pp) Quaker Outreach in Yorkshire 1994, 1997, 1999 A pocket-sized guide to Quaker acronyms, terms and expressions, committees and other bodies in Britain Yearly Meeting

Obtainable from:
Curlew Productions, Thirlestane House, Kelso TD5 8PD
Quakers in Britain; a century of change 1895-1995 (176 pp) Curlew Productions 1996. The only major publication to mark the centenary of the 1896 Manchester Conference, and to provide an evaluative study of the following 100 years.

The British Quakers 1647-1997 (44 pp) Curlew Productions 1997. This slim economical volume, abstracted from Quakers in Britain, is intended mainly for enquirers, attenders and new members.

Only one life: a Quaker's voyage (164 pp) Curlew Productions, 1998. [illustrated autobiography, 1915-1998].

Our Quaker Identity: Religious society – or friendly society. (64pp) Curlew Productions 1999. Reprinted 2000